T0129291

HOW TO PLAY THE HORSES— AND WIN

HOW TO PLAY THE HORSES— AND WIN

Robert Marshall

HOW TO PLAY THE HORSES—AND WIN

iUniverse books may be ordered through booksellers or by contacting:

iUniverse
1663 Liberty Drive
Bloomington, IN 47403
www.iuniverse.com
1-800-Authors (1-800-288-4677)

Because of the dynamic nature of the Internet, any web addresses or links contained in this book may have changed since publication and may no longer be valid. The views expressed in this work are solely those of the author and do not necessarily reflect the views of the publisher, and the publisher hereby disclaims any responsibility for them.

Any people depicted in stock imagery provided by Getty Images are models, and such images are being used for illustrative purposes only.
Certain stock imagery © Getty Images.

ISBN: 978-1-5320-8015-9 (sc)
ISBN: 978-1-5320-8016-6 (e)

Library of Congress Control Number: 2019911742

Print information available on the last page.

iUniverse rev. date: 08/12/2019

Thank you for being here with me. A good friend of mine used to say, "May the good horse be with you." I am saying, "May this book be with you."

This book is dedicated to all racing fans. Special thanks go to B, my best friend, who has stuck with me and given me massive support.

And to my son and daughters: whatever you want in life, you can get it if you try. And to my granddaughter, who seems like she will pass every test that she has been given and who shows no signs of fear.

Go cash that winning ticket.

HELLO! I AM HERE to help you make money when betting on horse racing.

Let me introduce myself. My name is Robert Marshall, and I am winning at horse racing at an 85 percent clip. You can do it too. I am not here to tell you a story about how my father was a horse player and used to send me to the offtrack betting (OTB) to place his bets. I am here to tell you how to win money by betting on horse racing. My father was a winner, but I believe it was luck, as he did not introduce me to the Daily Racing Form. He used to save the papers with the horses and jockeys, and then on race day he would look them over to find his winners. It worked for him.

There are so many things to look for when placing a bet. The first thing is to know your racetrack. But because I am a pro at betting on horse racing, I can choose any racetrack and still win.

As I said, my name is Marshall. And if you google the meaning of the name Marshall, you will see that it has something to do with horses—one who looks after horses or someone who cares for horses. But it has nothing to do with betting on horses. You have to learn that, and that is what this book is all about. I am going to teach you how to win. It is so simple, and I am going to teach you in the simplest way.

Now if you are reading this book, I know for sure that you are on your way to a winning streak. Yes! You are going to win like I do. After reading this book, you will finally be picking winners. I'm sure you never knew that it was so easy.

I've wanted to write this book because I see what lots of horse-racing handicappers are doing, and they are still not getting it right. Imagine how much bettors are losing by listening to those so-called handicappers who give out nothing but losers. They are more like actors to me. They don't know about the game. They love the game, like us, but they pick as though they are guessing.

Don't get me wrong. There are some really good horse-racing handicappers out there, but they won't let you in on their secrets.

They key to the game is to win, and if you are not winning, you need to continue reading this book. This book is going to change the way you play the game. Winning the game means not tearing up your tickets but rather cashing them in and putting money in your pocket. That is why I play this game. This is easy money.

I was losing and losing. Then I decided to change the way I played, and my winnings took off. I stick to my new ways, and that is what I am going to share with you.

Do you ever hang out at the track or at the sports book? There you can hear all different types of stories about how bettors found the winning horse for the race and did not play it. Instead they played the other horse, and the horse that they liked first beat the horse that they ultimately chose.

Or you might hear about the guy who had the Pick 3 or the Pick 4 and lost by one race because he did not have that extra horse on his ticket.

If you take your time and do your homework, you will cash that ticket. Sometimes all you have to do is pick that extra number and add just a few more dollars to your ticket. And that is what it's all about.

How many times do you find yourself in that situation? It used to happen to me until I learned how to win. You must play to win. It is not difficult to find winners if you know what to look for. Remember that you have the winners looking at you, saying, "Please pick me." Despite looking at the winner of the race, you pick the loser.

I believe that when you are gambling, you must wear your lucky colors at all times in order to keep the bad energy from you. A green candle is good for money, and a red candle keeps the negativity away. Personally, I like to wear a white T-shirt.

I am going to show you how to pick winners when betting on the horses. I have been playing the game since I was about fifteen years old. So now you can tell that betting on horse racing is in my blood.

But now I approach horse racing differently. I want to win and get paid, not just spend the whole day and walk away with nothing. Many guys just rip up the forms and jump on the bus. You must tell yourself that you want to win.

I was the type of kid who used to skip school just to be at the racetrack. It's so funny now to think back to when I used to jump on the train or the bus to get to the racetrack. And when the train was going too fast for me to jump off, I still jumped off and ended up hurting myself. My hands and knees would be all scratched up.

I used to get up early in the morning to go see the horses work out. I would get some good tips from the grooms. I liked to be around the grooms because they saw everything that happened at the track. Sometimes I brought them food or a good smoke.

Back in those days some grooms couldn't even buy a good pair of shoes. And when they gave me good picks, they expected me to help them out. Even now, there are still plenty of grooms who don't make much money. Any player who doesn't think that the groom knows more than the trainer about the horse needs to ask the trainer whether that is really true. The groom even has a better relationship with the jockey than the trainer does, so the groom is the marshal. And even when the groom knows that his horse is not going to win the race, he can let you know which horse or jockey is going to win.

One of my friends was a groom, and it was always fun to be around him because it gave me the chance to be around many horses both on and off the racetrack.

To be a real horse player, it has to be in your blood. You must eat, sleep, and dream about it. Back in my hometown of Jamaica, the races were twice a week, Wednesday and Saturday.

The racetrack was school for me, and Saturdays were holidays. That was how I learned about horses and how they ran. But I still did not know the game. I was winning by getting tips. I was around the right people at the right time, but I did not know what handicapping was.

There are some pretty good jockeys and trainers from Jamaica who are currently active and winning races in the United States. You can find one of my favorite trainers at Gulfstream Park in Florida, and he is still winning races. And a few jockeys from Jamaica are winning for their Jamaican connection. When you see them, don't overlook them.

I was only playing with luck back in those days. Yes, I was lucky to be around major jockeys and trainers. That was until someone showed me the Daily Racing Form. It's a big magazine with the names of the trainers, owners, jockeys, and horses, with all kinds of numbers. I didn't know how to read it, and I never saw my father with a copy, so I didn't think it was interesting.

With horse racing, every step of the way must be approached with patience. Don't rush to put in that bet, or you might end up ripping that bet up. There will always be other races on which to bet.

Sometimes you will see a guy running to get up to the ticket window to place his bet, and after the race he rips up his ticket and dumps it in the trash. I never bet on the first race, unless I am going to start a fifty-cent Pick 5. I use that first race to see how the track is going to play out for that day and to see which jockey has momentum. Sometimes the jockey or trainer who won the first race ends up having a glory day. So that jockey or trainer is yours to watch for the day. He could win three races that day. But if you are a first-race double player, more power to you.

Back in the day I used to focus on a particular jockey/ trainer combination, and any time I saw that combination in a race, I would pick them. My racing friends would do the same. As a matter of fact, our nickname would be that particular jockey's name.

Horse betting is a skill. It is more than just what you see on paper. The horse might look so good on paper that it makes you want to sell your house. You could just bet on it, but then what if that horse doesn't even place?

Sometimes, you might start to chase your money. Never chase the money, even though sometimes you might get lucky. I know a kid who was betting the whole day and could not cash a ticket. He said that he was either going home broke or going home with some money in his pocket. He asked a few of us for a few dollars, something that I wouldn't give him. But he got the money and hit the last race, which paid him over two grand at the Santa Anita racetrack.

Some guys started to count all the change that was in their pockets to see if they could come up with another bet. When you finish reading this book, you won't have to do that, because I don't do that, and I cannot beat the bookies all by myself. So I am here to show you how I do it.

As I am writing this book, I am in a Las Vegas sports book, winning. What better way for me to write this book for you!

When I play, I put money in my pocket. You must bet to win, no matter how you play the game. You must box your bet at all times if you come up with more than one horse that you think has a chance to win the race.

It is better to add a number to your ticket than to take one off. I saw guys do that and then sing about how they picked the winner of the race and dropped it from their ticket. I just hit the Pick 4. Easy money in my pocket, and all I spent was nine dollars. I am going to show you how I handicap, and the first winnings you get will make this book free. I know for sure that the money you pay for this book is going to multiply. And you must spread the good news that you finally bought a book that taught you how to win at the races.

There are two ways to look for winners: one is to read the Daily Racing Form, and the other is to be at the track. When you are at the track, you must know what you are looking for. You must look at the horses to see how they are acting.

I was at a certain racetrack, and everyone was betting on horse number six as the public choice. Horse six was going off at a 6–5 favorite. But when the horse came out into the paddock, he was bandaged all over his four legs. What do you think happened? The horse finished last, and you could not see that in the Daily Racing Form. But I saw it and bet against it. I did my homework. That horse was not a single, and moreover my numbers were higher than his.

If you don't know by now that horse racing is a numbers game, then you are on the right track. Unless you are playing with luck and the luck runs out, your losing streak begins. I used to feel sick when I had a losing streak, and I blamed it on everyone around me. But now it is a new ball game. Now friends call me to ask me who I like in particular races. When I say, "Go set it," they know what I mean.

Speed has a lot to do with the outcome of the race, but you must know how to make your own Beyer Speed Figure by looking at what trouble the horse ran into during the running of the race. Bettors like to play horses with the most speed, but most horses don't run two races alike. A horse will probably run better on his second time out. If a horse ran an 81, then next time out he will come up with a 75. The 75 is going to be his last Beyer Speed Figure, so if he caught a race with horses doing 60s and 70s, that horse can run back his 81 and win the race.

And if a horse ran an 85 Beyer Speed Figure, and he is on the rail or, say, in the middle of the track, and the other horse ran a 79, but he ran wide, block, and faltered, you can adjust that 79.

When reading the Daily Racing Form, you must look for everything that the horse did the last time he raced.

I am tired of seeing those so-called handicappers who dress in suits and ties and give out losing horses every race day. They do it for fun. Yes, they are on the internet and on TV. If you are still listening to them, that means you are losing just like them. Don't waste time on those guys. They are getting paid to make you lose.

I was watching a YouTube video about how those guys play on a bettor's mentality. If it was a two-horse race, and they said bet on number one, I would bet on number two. But when you finish reading this book, you won't need to waste time with them. Instead, you will do your own handicapping, and you'll cash those winning tickets.

I can't believe that so many handicappers handicap the Kentucky Derby and did not pick Justify to win. Please! What did you not see? He was clearly the better horse in the race.

My number show that his is a walk over. A lock of the day. Yes, they were telling you how the number fourteen horse was going to win because he won big in his country. But after I combed the horse, I knew for sure that he was going to burn a lot of money.

First things first, the horse that he beat by 18.5 ran down the track in the oaks. That was a big sign, and the handicapper did not see that. The horse was sweating all over, and when it came out on the racetrack, it was jumping, showing that it did not like the mud.

And what about his trainer? Did you not see his numbers for a dirt track?

Let us salute Justify, who has shown how great he is. Now he is retired and is living a wonderful life. An undefeated Triple Crown winner, he started out by winning a maiden special. Then he moved up and won an allowance in great style. That was the test when the connection decided to put him in the Santa Anita Derby.

Yes, he passed the test by winning, and now the connection knows what kind of horse they got. The next move is to ship him to Kentucky. This move is going to have the world of horse racing paying attention.

Some said that the Kentucky Derby was way out of his reach, but the horse did not think so. He won the Derby.

Most of the time, the horse that wins the Kentucky Derby comes back to win the Preakness. The Belmont was the main concern. With no introduction, the Preakness came up, and the track was muddy—just what the doctor ordered.

Justify won the Preakness. The next move was to get the horse to the Belmont. This was going to be the final leg of the Triple Crown and maybe the final race for Justify.

As you probably know, Belmont is a longer distance, and some trainers want to give their horses a rest so that they can run better. Some skip the Preakness and wait for the Belmont. But there was no rest for Justify. This was the race that he had to win. Justify won the Belmont and became the Triple Crown winner.

Some bettors go to the windows and get stuck. They just don't know what they are doing or on whom they want to bet.

You should know what bets you are going to make before you go to the window. Give the other guy a chance to place his bets. You don't want to take a whole day to handicap and still not know whom to bet on.

Now sports books hang a sign that reads, "No handicapping while you are at the windows."

Follow your first instinct if you can't make up your mind. When I wrote this book, I was thinking about you. This book is going to make it easy for you to pick winners. And if you stick to this book, you are going to see and pick those long shots. When you see those long shots, do not second-guess yourself. Go for it. And with those long shots you should pick up a pretty good pay, when you are playing the trifecta and the superfecta.

A guy was making the loudest noise, cheering his horse to the winning post at 50–1, but when he went to cash the ticket, he noticed that the ticket in his hand was for a different track. I felt bad for the guy. You must always check your tickets before you leave the window.

But things happen. A long time ago, a jockey by the name of Purple was riding a horse that was going to pay big on that racing day. Her agent was Angel. We all liked the horse, and it was going to pay off at 40–1. Purple was told to go out there, make the horse relax, and then make that big move. The gate opened, and they were off. At the front was Purple, up by two to three lengths. As she turned for home, she was all alone at 40–1, and we started to celebrate. We were loud, and as the horse approached the winning post, Purple fell off the horse. It looked like she just jumped off and burned my money. I was sick inside and promised to never bet on Purple again. She said the horse jumped from its own shadow.

Back in the day, when I didn't know how to read the Daily Racing Form, I looked through it. But I wasn't looking for certain things. It would take me the whole racing day to figure it out.

I was not winning. I could not understand why a horse would win by ten lengths on race day. When the horse raced the next time around, he finished down the track. I thought a horse winning like that was a sure bet the next time out, but it doesn't always work like that. The horse might be stepping up in class or just feel like he doesn't want to run on that day. It's just like us. One day we'll have a winning day, and then come tomorrow we just can't find a winning horse. It can happen to anyone.

I once took someone to the racetrack on a day that I thought I was going to win a lot of money. But that day I could not pick a winner. My friend was having the kind of day that I was dreaming of having. She had great winnings. I was reading the Daily Racing Form like any handicapper would do, and she was just picking numbers. She was winning, and I was losing. She said that the horse was looking at her. Every horse that looked at her was winning that day. By the time I started to see what was really happening, the horses stopped looking.

There are so many ways to win. Some people like to look at the horses' colors. Some play their birthdays and license plates. Some play names also. If I see my name, yes, I am going to bet on it. My sister's name wins all the time. I bet on her name when I see it and get lucky. Sometimes If I see a name like Bud, Weed, or Smoke, I am going to bet on that horse.

One night I was at the Vegas sports book, betting on horses. Night racing can be tough to handicap. I was down until I saw a horse named Smoking. I just lit one up, and that was a perfect time for me. And you know what? Smoking won the race. I made my money back. I did not win a lot, but

I made my money back. I left the sports book even. But that was then. Now that I can read the Daily Racing Form, things have changed. I am now winning 85 percent of my bets.

Whenever you play the game, the first thing to look for in the Daily Racing Form is the condition of the race. That is very important. It will show you the flow of the race. The condition of the race will point out which horses you need to throw out and which ones are going to compete very well.

You should also look for trainers and jockey combinations. The purse money is important, so don't forget to look back at the price of the race. That is what the horses are racing for. We, as the bettors, are betting on odds. Trainers want a piece of that purse money.

Some jockeys do not win cheap races. If the race is a cheap claimers, then you should look for a bug. Hot Apprentice win those type of races and they pay a big price too. The reason is that they are getting a weight break. And they are overlooked in the wager.

One night I was playing at Charles Town racetrack. I saw the muddy track, with only five horses in the race. The longest shot went off at 50–1 with a bug name as the rider. His horse was carrying the lightweight, and the horse won the race. I did not see that coming.

I like to play West Coast tracks, Santa Anita and Del Mar. But I like the Belmont and Gulfstream racetracks also.

With the way I handicap, I can play out at any racetrack. Because I know what to look for, I am, in turn, making it easy for you.

Some bettors believe that maiden claiming races are very difficult to handicap, but again you must look for trainers who love to play the claiming game and bet on them—not because a horse may look good on paper, but because the horse is going to win. You have to take the trainer's claiming percentage into consideration. I see it all the time—a horse is a betting favorite in a claiming race, but the trainer is about 50–3 in a claiming race. The trainer ends up sending out fifty horses to race, and only three win. His chances of winning are very low, so I am looking for a horse to beat his.

Look for horses that are dropping with good form. Also look at the price for which the horse was purchased. Some bettors like to look at how much money a horse made at his preferred grounds and distance, which can help, as well. A horse can be dropping with a dull form, but drop in his right spot and meet his kind. Take notice of that kind of drop. That horse can win the race.

A trainer might change the jockey. Just because a jockey used to ride a certain horse and then chooses to ride a different horse in the race doesn't mean that the former horse has no chance. Some jockeys have contracts to ride certain horses. One particular jockey rode Eloweasel and Noble Freud but chose to ride Noble Freud in the race. Eloweasel won the race at 9–1, but the public went for a jockey change to win the race.

I saw horses drop from 20,000 to 10,000 and pay forty dollars to win. The horse might not be showing good form, but you can't overlook a drop like that. Again, the horse can be fit and ready to win, so the trainer steps the horse up in class and gets a win. Only certain trainers do that, so you must know them when they make that move. Maiden claiming and claiming races are the same to me. The main reason is that those horses are up for sale. It is the best way to get a horse for less than the purchase price. Or maybe the trainer has too many horses and wants to get the stable smaller. When handicapping a straight maiden race, the first thing I look for is the owner or trainer. Then I look at the quality of the horse and see how the trainers are working the horse. Big trainers want to win at first asking.

Not every trainer likes to work their horses fast, unless it is Bob T. If a trainer has a really good horse, he is going to call for his go-to jockey. The same thing goes for two-year-olds. Some trainers don't work their horses fast, but they can get the win at good odds. Some horse's dam has won at first asking, so his horses can win at first asking too. Don't overlook that.

Distance is another factor. You cannot overlook that a horse will like more than one distance, but only master one. Some horses that love a wet track will also like turf. A horse that loves a firm turf will also like a fast track. When betting on a turf race, look for trainers who do very well on that surface. And do the same for jockeys. Not any jockey can win on the turf, especially those 6 1/2 downhill or a mile and 1/8. Any turf races over a mile and 1/16. I try to see which horse is going to be the closer. And with a good jockey, I might be celebrating early.

Again, some jockeys are great in sprint races, so when you see a good jockey in a sprint race, don't overlook him.

You might see horses in a race in which they have no business to be. Maybe the connection just likes to waste money. It is not cheap to keep a horse in a stable, plus you have to pay to nominate a horse in a race. But I guess some trainers just love the game or are in it to get bounced around. Or perhaps they are racing for fourth money so they can collect on the superfecta or the high 5. You won't see them in my win section of the bet.

Some guys bet on these horses to win. I don't know what they see in them. Some of these horses take money and don't even place. When handicapping a Pick 3–6, you can easily draw a line through them and throw them out.

Allowance races are for horses that are not good for stake races. Trainers race them where they are fit to race. And if the horse cannot win, the next time you see the horse, it might be wearing a For Sale tag.

Many horses try stakes after a Md Sp Wt. Win but drop back down to right level. Those moved should be approached very carefully, because although you might think that move is a drop down in class, that's where the horse belongs. Horses like that usually sell favorite and run down the track.

Another foolish transaction I see burn a lot of money is when first-time winners bet against winners. That means that the horse just beat a field of no winners and now has to face horses that have already won races. If you draw a line through those horses, it can make your handicapping easier.

One of the worst moves that I've seen in the racing industry is the gelding game. Now put yourself in that situation. If you were to be gelded today, how long would it take for you to heal? Do you think that you could be up in two days and be running? I couldn't. I would be sour and in pain. Gelding a horse can make the horse run better or run worse. They say that the horse does not feel pain after twenty-four hours. But I'm going to teach you what I know about gelding and racing a horse in terms of handicapping. Some players love to bet on first-time gelding. But how many first-time geldings do you see winning races? Some trainers geld their horses before they reach two. Most of the time, those horses don't win much. To me, the best time to geld a horse is at three. You will get more wins from that horse.

Whenever you see a first-time gelding race, you must check for the date that the horse was gelded. The date is at the top of the Daily Racing Form, where it tells you if the horse is a colt or a mare.

The next thing you'll want to know is whether the trainer worked the horse after the gelding. If the trainer did not work the horse and is going to race the horse, that horse is not going to win. If the trainer gave the horse a rest after the gelding and then worked him, and the work became better than before the geld, that horse can be a sure winner. Don't just bet on a horse because you see a first-time gelding. Make sure you pay attention.

For the players who like to play half track, those track with the quarter horse's race. Sometimes you may see a race with gelding mares racing together. I've seen fillies beat up those geldings.

If a horse won and paid big money, and you did not get on the first win, and you see the horse is racing in an upcoming race, don't waste your money on a bet. Most of the time those horses don't win back. The same goes for those older horses, those 23–1 and upward. It is simple. If a horse took twenty-three times to win a race, that horse might take another twenty-three times before taking the next picture. Yet bettors still burn money on those horses. When I see them, I draw a line through them so that I can narrow down my selection.

Some trainers race for feeding money, so be careful where you place those horses. I have great respect for Bob and Mike, so you know that jockey-and-trainer combination is gold. When you are handicapping, that is something for which you should look.

Every trainer has a favorite jockey. When I am playing New York tracks, I look to see who Chad or Cher is racing. They've won a lot of races together. Always watch the jockeys and trainers. These are just two hot trainers of so many.

Make sure you study. Notice what is happening every race day. Know which day certain trainers and jockeys are winning. If a certain jockey does not win on Sunday, it is easy for me to rule him out. You can find some long shots that way. It is only right to do so. I look for everything that can make me a winner. I also look up the jockey's or trainer's birthday. Jockeys and trainers will want to celebrate their birthdays on the track. What better way to do so than to win a few races.

If you have a gambling problem, you should seek help. Don't gamble your bill money. You must gamble with responsibility. Some guys don't know when to stop. They gamble their paychecks and put their families in the dark. If you don't pay the bookie, you might lose a leg. Don't do it.

One of the best ways to win money in horse racing is to form a syndicate. That way you can have more chances to win Pick 6 and other competitions. But don't wait for the pot to reach up in the hundreds of thousands before you play. At the end there might be more winners, and you might get a lower payoff than what you put in. My friends put up a $3,000 bet in a Pick 6 carryover that would reach up to $1.2 million. They hit the Pick 6, but the pay was a little over $600.

In this case there were too many winners to share the money. If they had waited for a different race day, they would have collected a cool $20,000 or $30,000.

Did you know that there are jockeys who give signals to their friends while in the parade ring? Yes, they do. They also do it when coming out on the track. One day I was at the track, and after the trainer gave his jockey instructions on how to ride the horse, the jockey mounted the horse, and when he was in the parade ring, he hit his number with his whip. That was the jockey's way of telling someone that his horse was ready. The horse didn't win every time, but for sure the horse was going to run. The horse won the race. Sometimes the jockey might stand tall in the saddle. Look, and you will notice these things.

Who said that the mobs are not a part of the game? When a race is fixed, who do you think is fixing it? News travels fast, and if a jockey was told to put his horse in traffic or take his horse wide, you'll know. Jockeys are very good at placing the horse where they want it to be. If they want to stick behind the horse, they can. And if they want to take the horse wide, they can.

I was watching a race where the number three was the second speed in the race, with a favorite at 6–5. Before the race, the number three bolted through the gate. Now they scratched the number three, and the favorite became 1–9. The other speed went wire to wire, and the favorite finished dead last. Don't you believe that the race was fixed?

I live in Las Vegas, and back in the day there was talk of the "good old boy" syndrome. I love the Vegas casinos. Red was the man then. He was well dressed, as if he was the owner of the sports book. He was winning every bet. His tips were coming to him. Any time that he got on his phone, I knew that he had the winner of the race. I tried to get close to him so that I could see who he was betting on. But I knew that Red did not like to see me. He never liked to see someone dressed better than he was, or he thought that I was there to rob him. He got paranoid when he saw me. His brother would tell him that I was just there to bet and not to worry about me. He was right. I was only there to win some money and have a great time. I thought everyone was just like me and wanted to help beat the bookie. I could not do it by myself.

Back in the day I won on new luck. I never disrespected Red. I liked the guy's style. One day I was in the Vegas casino and I heard all this commotion. When I went to see what was happening, Red was lying on his back. He had fallen and couldn't get up. He was having a heart attack. His horse got nipped on the wire. I didn't know how much he bet, but that knocked him down.

Some guys can bet big bucks, but while watching the race their hearts race. I don't believe those guys should be playing the game.

The ambulance came to take Red to the hospital. I made sure that Red saw me standing over him so that the next time he saw me, his way of thinking about me would have changed. And it worked. Now when he sees me, we exchange conversation. The heart attack gave him strokes, so now when you see Red, he has tubes with oxygen in his nose. And he is still betting on winners.

I also met Long John at the Vegas casino. Long John is a very good handicapper. He came from Chicago with big dreams and money. Any time you are at the track and you see a 5–4 play, you can bet that Long John has a ticket in his pocket.

Gambling is not a sure thing, and no matter how well you think you know the game, there are going to be times when the horse is not going to meet your expectations (unless you bet every horse that is in the race). Jockeys make wrong moves, and those can cause them the race.

It's always fun to be at the Vegas casino. It is one of my favorite places to be. A nice tall waitress used to work there. She was very friendly and always made sure that we get our drinks. She was a one-of-a-kind good luck charm.

The Vegas casino was the place to be. The people were very nice, and the food was very good. This was where all the old-timers came and talked about their good old days. And when they closed down the casino, we all moved to the other place across the street, now called the sports book. It was better for horse playing, but now it seems like they don't like horse racing. The waitress complains that they are not making much money since they changed the drinks rule. Some sports books in Vegas want you to spend ten or twenty units before you can get a drink ticket. I am not saying that you must drink and play the game, but you can get away with sticking a dollar in a penny slot machine. Once the waitress sees you are playing, she will ask you what kind of drink you want. My favorite sports books to play the horses are the Station Casinos. At Texas Station or Palace Station you might see me cashing my winnings. Very nice people work at all the Station Casinos. The waitress will keep coming back to take your drink order, and you do not need a drink ticket. As long as you are playing the horses, your drinks are free. All you have to do is keep tipping the waitress, and she will keep coming back. My favorite is the short one. If you are at Texas Station, say hi to her, and you will get a smile.

Now all the old-timers are at the other casino. It is not the same as the Vegas casino or the one across the street, but they will still take your bets, and when you win, you get paid. We didn't like the casino that is across the street. To us it was too much of a change, and it was more about football than horse racing. So now we go to the Station Casinos. Any one will do.

If you ever come up on a race and you just can't find the winning horse, it has "long shot" written all over it. Then you can press the *all* button and find your single somewhere else. Bet with your gut. That 35–1 long shot will give you a juicy payoff.

Be careful how you bet on those first-time geldings. Check how the horse works on the track after the gelding. If the horse works slowly, it was not a very successful gelding. But if the horse works fast and the trainer adds equipment, that horse could be a single.

I am hoping that this book will be ready for the Breeders' Cup. But even if it doesn't make it on time, it will be ready when you are ready to make some money. Where are all my horse players? We were born to love this sport. It is the best sport in the whole wide world.

I saw Black, and he looked like a mess. He is one of the old-timers who used to play at the Vegas casino. He knows how to pick winners. As a matter of fact, he is the one who started me in playing the Pick 4. But sometimes when you hear Black talk, you don't know if he is lying or telling the truth. A lady is always looking for him. And Black loves to talk and joke about everything he knows. Everyone loves Black. He is a nice guy. You will always see him and his partner together. They like to play the Pick 4.

If you see the final race of the day, and Black is still sitting down, that means he has a ticket to cash. That is the best feeling in horse racing.

Watching your horse crossing the winning post causes a good feeling, but cashing that winning ticket delivers a great feeling. I cash a lot of winning tickets on shippers. Trainers ship their horses from coast to coast to get a win. And when they take their jockeys along with them, they really mean business. They may not win, but they come for a piece of the pie. Again, some trainers are masters of shipping. If you see them ship a horse to your main track, don't overlook it. The horse may fit enough to pay you all.

Overseas shippers love the turf, and you must pay special attention to those horses, especially when they are going long distances. Those horses are used to carrying heavy weight, and they race with big field. When they are shipped here, they race with less weight. Not all of them are good, so you must look at their form and the Timeform rating.

Overseas horses, like European horses, have a Timeform rating. If the rating is below 100, I don't waste time on them, unless they are maiden and are on the turf. Most of the time those horses are shipped over, and trainers place them in the wrong spot. They are often placed in grade stakes races. Some of them will win if their numbers are over 100.

One day I was playing at a track, when I saw a shipper with a 116 Timeform rating two races down. He was not in a stake race. He was in an allowance race with a top jockey in the iron. The horse won and paid thirty dollars to win. Horses like that will light up the Pick 4, and you will smile big.

There are many ways to wager on the horses. You can do the win, place, or show. "Win" is when the horse wins the race. "Place" is when the horse either wins or comes in second. And "show" is when the horse comes in first, second, or third. Then you have the exacta, which is just what it sounds like. The first two horses must finish in first and second place. And if you like two horses in the race, you can box the bet and be on the safe side. For example, say you play 1–2 exacta, and the race finishes 2–1. By boxing the bets, you will still get paid. But if you don't box the bet, then you have to rip up that ticket.

The trifecta pays more than the exacta, but your horse must win, along with the horse that came in second plus the horse that finished third. There are many ways that you can play a trifecta. You can key your favorite horse and add a few more horses to it that you know will finish second and third. But in this case, the key horse has to win. If you don't know for sure, then box the bet. Once I find the exacta, I am going to box the exacta and go for the trifecta. This is the way I play the trifecta: I box 1 and 2, then make my guesses for 3, 4, and 5. And this bet only costs you 3 units.

The superfecta pays more than the trifecta, but now you need your horses to run in order of first, second, third, and fourth. This play costs more units but is not necessary. If you are going to play the trifecta, you might as well go for the superfecta and hope to find a long shot that can be a real payoff. I love to play a good long shot. You have to dig deep to find them. Picking a long shot is like going to the Vegas strip clubs and leaving with a happy ending.

The trifecta and the superfecta will have you winning the big money. Or you can go for the Pick 3, 4, 5, and 6. To win, you have to get all the combinations you wagered.

When I play the Pick 4, I like to play the last four races on the program. But I handicap the last race first because that is the getaway race. I make sure I spend more time with that race because I don't want to miss anything.

I heard a while back that some men had robbed a bank, and they had not planned their getaway. They got caught, and they all lost.

My next race to handicap is going to be the first race that starts the Pick 4. This race is the spotting race. The Pick 4 cannot start without this race. This is a must-win race. You have to spot this race very carefully. Most of the time this kind of race becomes a claimer or a Md. Sp Wt. You must go with everything that you've learned so far. This is a race where anything can happen. The moment you overlook something, it will get you.

The next two races are a must-win situation. And one of these races might be a stake race. That is my next race to handicap. Most of the time the big jockeys and big trainers win these types of races. With one more race to handicap, I have my Pick 4. I feel very good about my picks, and I am ready to go put in my bets.

If you are confident about your Pick 4, you can just go for the Pick 5 and win some more money. One race up is the start of the Pick 5. I have to take my chances. I am going for the Pick 5. If I believe that I have a great chance of winning the Pick 4, why not take some more time and find the winner of this race? Now I can bet the Pick 5 and the Pick 4 and get that money.

Now my mind is singing. There is still more money out there to win. I know that I am going to win the Pick 4 and the Pick 5, but what about the Pick 6? There is big money in the Pick 6 pool. One race up is the beginning of the Pick 6. Go for it, and cash those winning tickets.

How would you feel if you needed just one more winner in order to collect the Pick 6, and the jockey jumped off the horse and turned for home? That can happen. Or you know that there's no way the favorite is going to win the last race, so you bet against it, only to find out that they scratched your horse and gave you the favorite. The favorite did not lift a foot, and you lost your ticket.

We have another Triple Crown winner. Justify was way too good for his competition. Can you believe that a lot of handicappers were saying that the horse wasn't going to win the race? The horse proved them wrong. Justify got what he needed, and that was the fast track. He had the fastest speed figure in the race for the fast track. Even though his last speed was 97, the Beyer Speed Figure was 109. This racing game is about numbers, and the Daily Racing Form is packed with them.

Other websites will give you a handicapper edge. I like brisnet.com. It puts together a lot of information about speed and pace ratings. Not every handicapper knows how to read the speed and pace ratings. Again, when you know how to read those numbers and put them together, I bet that you are going to pick more winners.

Another website that I use is TimeformUS.com. It tells you more about pace. It shows you where your horses should be in a race. Unless the jockey decides to do something else, the numbers predict where the horse should be early or late in the race. All early and late numbers correspond to the distance of the race. For example, if a race is going five furlongs, and the TimeformUS is early 114, and late is 57 or little higher, I look to see which horse in the race is close to an early 114. If not, then I know that that horse is the lone speed and they are not going to catch him. But if it is a longer race, seven furlongs or longer, then I know that the horse is going to stop.

Now I am going to look for a late high number, which is a closer to run him down and win the race. This could be tricky because if the TimeformUS is a low 50 early and a 114 late going 7 furlongs or a mile, he might be coming too late and end up just for a share. But if you are getting a mile and an eighth and more, then you cannot overlook that. I love to handicap those long-distance races, and it doesn't matter if they are on the turf or on dirt. Pace and speed have a lot to do with long-distance races and even sprints.

If you go to brisnet.com, you will see the pace speed formula. If the pace is high and the speed is low, that is going to the lead horse. When you see the pace is low and the speed is high, then you know that is a closer. If a race is going long and you see a pace of 79 and a speed of 92, with a clean trip the horse will be coming. But if you see a pace of 102 and a speed of 80 or more, and the next closest pace is 90 or less, that means that he is gone. I told you that this is a numbers game, so if you can put them rightly together, you are going to win most of the time.

If you look back at Justify's early and late numbers, there is no way you could have said that he wasn't going to win the Belmont. Let me remind you that Justify's early number was 127. His late number was 85. The horse that finished second was a shipper with a Timeform rating of over 100.

You must give this serious consideration. Horse numbers will excel on his track. When putting your numbers together, you must look for the horses for the course and the distance specialists. Some horses just don't like to win away from home. And if you see that the jockey put up a number and took the ride back, you know that his number might improve or remain the same. And if your numbers are close to each other, then you can take a look at the weight. If you are betting on a five-furlong turf race, and you see a horse with a Beyer Speed Figure of 75 and up, and the other horse is showing a pace and speed figure, bet on the one that is showing only the Beyer

Speed Figure. It will also work for horses that are going four and a half furlong.

I don't watch the Beyer Speed Figure when picking my winners. I am not saying that you shouldn't, but horses don't run the same numbers, and most of the time horses bounce, especially in two-year-old races. I saw the horse come out and run a big Beyer. Then the next time out, the public bet the horse down. And the horse got beat. I see it all the time. If you are betting on two-year-old maidens, and you see the pace number is high and the speed number is high, that horse is going to bounce.

I like to get my form overnight. That way I can put enough time into this. For me this is work, and when you put in a good day of work, you are bound to get paid. A good friend of mine loves to play the game, and he loves to give me some good long shots. He's always giving me good horses that he likes. He says, "Hey, I see this horse that I like. It'll race tomorrow, and the price will be right." I ask, "Why do you like that horse?" His reply is that he has been watching that horse for a while, and he believes it is time for the horse to win.

I am still waiting for him to give me a winning horse. I don't care if it only pays fifty cents on the dollar. I just want to pick a winner. (He promised to buy the very first copy of this book.)

The speed figure is a very important factor. It tells you how hard a horse gallops at a certain distance. It also points out a horse's best distance. And you'll know if a horse is going to bounce. When I am looking for winners, I always take into account the speed figure. It takes a lot of work to add all the horses' speed figures in every race. And I like to add the last three times that the horse raced. If a horse is racing for the first time after his age change, and he is working well, he is going to run harder than the way he left, and his number should go up.

Some horses win right after an age change, while some take forever. I like to see the number that the horse went on the shelf with, so when it comes back to racing, the horse doesn't beat that number. Then I know if the horse is ready. For example, if the horse leaves with an 85 Beyer Speed Figure, comes back running, and gets less than 85, I know right away that the horse did not make a good age change. And the next time the horse races, the number still sticks under 85. I know that no matter what the trainers do, that horse is not going to beat his 85 Beyer Speed Figure. So now I must look elsewhere for the winning horse. A horse can run one and one-sixteenth, and one and one-eighth and still show the same speed figure for both distances, while the Beyer Speed Figure does not show that. I see the Beyer Speed Figure with an 88–90, but when you check the speed figure, the number is a 98–98. You can tell that the horse is going to run back a 98 or less.

If the other horses in the race run less than a 98, then you know that your 98 can win. Only two things can happen: either the horse repeats that 98, or it bounces.

You should never predict that a horse is going to bounce until it happens. I used to make that mistake, but I've paid to learn. Now when I see a horse put up his numbers and is winning, I stay with it. I do not bet against it. I don't bet for a horse to bounce.

Now this is where you will find the Speed Figure in the Daily Racing Form. After the odds on what the horse went off at, there are numbers like 83–15. Now when you add those two numbers, you will get 98. That is your Speed Figure.

Your Daily Racing Form is packed with information, but many people overlook much of it.

Your TimeformUS number is under the jockey's name. It is a very good resource to help you pick your winning horses.

I use the Tomlinson Ratings only when there's a wet track and the turf race moves to dirt. It points out the horses that are suited for the wet track and distance. But it does not work all the time. Some bettors love to look for gray horses with big feet. The Tomlinson shows you numbers instead of horse names. For example, instead of seeing a horse's name (for example, Holy Bull), you would see the horse's numbers for a wet track displayed like this: Wet (428). That is a high number for a wet track. Then you want to look at the distance, according to the race. A distance of 364 is a high number for a horse to win on a wet track. That is how the Tomlinson works. But some jockeys don't like to ride on wet tracks.

The jockey knows that the inside track is sloppy and heavy, so it is best to have the horse on the outside. If the jockey has the best horse, it shouldn't be a problem doing that. The jockey goes to the lead, opens up by three, and grabs the dead rail. Doesn't he know how the track is playing? He just rode two races back. Anyway, a horse comes on the outside and blows past him.

These things happen all the time. But if you put the Tomlinson and the speed figure together, you can cash a pretty good ticket.

Just like with the Beyer Speed Figure, if a horse shows a number for turf and is racing on dirt, you cannot use that number unless that horse is making a big dropdown in class.

Every horse has its best numbers for distance and surfaces. But you already know that. Nothing is a sure bet. Even though the numbers might be right, and the trainer's horse is ready for that big run, if the horse doesn't want to run that day, you cannot make it run.

I have this horse as a good bet, and it's supposed to win and have me collect. But the gate opens, and there he is, still standing at the gate. You cannot handicap that.

Another massive play that you must look out for is trainer angles. Trainers like to stick to what works for them. Certain trainers are very good at their first time at the route, or when restarting their careers. When I look for a certain winner, I pay attention to certain plays.

Some handicappers see them after the race, and they start to sing about how they did not see the move before the race. Some trainers like to do the turf-to-dirt, dirt-to-turf, or first-time-turf dance. Some trainers pay good dividends making those moves. What about off layoff move? There is so much more to dance to, so please don't overlook anything. A horse's first time with a trainer can come at a price. Some trainers know how to wake those horses and have them running.

Don't ever look past a blinker's move. Even though your horse trainers can be very good at what they do, sometimes they can have a very cold meet.

Focus on the hot trainers, as they can give you the edge. I look at the Daily Racing Form for the trainer standing, which is where I can see the leading trainers and jockeys. There you can see who is hot and who is not.

Another important factor you must consider is the winning post position. You might not realize how important this is. Before I started to use it, I was picking horses to win at certain post positions, but they didn't. When I started to follow up on where the horses drew, my winnings started to improve. I liked a horse that was going a mile on the turf. He drew post position ten, with a very good jockey on him. The horse did not win. He came in second, beaten by a length. But when I went back and looked at the winning post positions, number ten on the turf going a mile is 0–21. If I had seen that earlier,

I wouldn't have played number 10 to win. It is very important to give the winning post positions a good look.

As I write this, I am playing at Santa Anita and drinking some beer. I am looking forward to playing at Del Mar. It is a very nice track in the summer.

Finally, whenever you are looking for your winners, don't forget to look at where they've been bred. Most handicappers like to bet on Kentucky breeds. But it depends on the shape of the race. I like to bet Kentucky breeds against New York breeds anytime. Even though I play the West Coast tracks most of the time, I can win at any racetrack.

This book will certainly have you step up your winnings. Combine what you've learned with what you are already doing, and become the best handicapper ever. This is money in your pocket.

Printed in the United States
By Bookmasters